Special Warfare: An Adoption Story

A Story About Doug Vanderford's Adoption and Life Purpose that Led Him to Navy's Special Warfare Combatant-Craft Crewman (SWCC)

Douglas Vanderford and Elena Lee

NumenPremium.com

ISBN: 9798368036731

Cover Designed By: Sean Cordes

Special Warfare Combat Crewman (SWCC)

Who Are We

"Navy SWCC support and perform maritime special operations in open ocean, littoral and riverine environments. Their professional occupation in the Navy is known as Special Warfare Boat Operator (SB). SBs are experts in maritime special operations tactics and missions; foreign cultural awareness; advanced weapons tactics; tactical communications; tactical air control; tactical ground mobility; small arms and crew-served weapons; fast roping and rappelling; advanced craft operations; long-range, over the horizon, and riverine navigation; tactical combat medicine and trauma care; intelligence operations; and chemical, biological, radiological, or nuclear defense measures; among others"

- *Naval Special Warfare*

Throughout the book, phrases from Navy Sea, Air, and Land (SEAL) teams and Special Warfare Combatant-Craft Crewman SWCC were incorporated into the story line. A SWCC symbol denotes the "easter egg"/phrase used among the elite.

ACKNOWLEDGMENTS

Special Thanks = those who have somehow "brought something" into life that has meaning to me.

Adoption involves multiple factors – my "experience" was fortunate. Acquired by the only parents I have ever known Charles & Diane Vanderford – THANK YOU! To my biological mother/father/brothers/sisters I may or may not have, THANK YOU! To my 2 former X "Y's" (marriages), both relationships produced valued memories and two children, THANK YOU! To Ms. E – the author/friend/colleague whom through writing her first in the series of adoption stories, Coming to America: An Adoption Story – her book is the motivator bringing my story to print – THANK YOU! And finally, to my "domestic partner" the one we believe to have received the message, by going through our previous "mess" – Lisa, THANK YOU!

It is also just as important for me to say THANK YOU to all my current and former brothers and sisters from other mothers who have served our country. There truly is nothing like a heart of a volunteer – especially a heart of those who choose to pay the ultimate sacrifice for our country, THANK YOU!

Final Note: THANK YOU! The individuals who have chosen to purchase/ receive this unique capture of moments from my personal adoption story. If it motivates you or someone else to discuss the unyielding benefits of literally saving a life, then this journey is worthwhile.

Ride your ride! Keep pushing the skinny pedal on the right! On time, On target, NEVER Quit!

V/r

Douglas S. Vanderford

CONTENTS

Special Warfare: An Adoption Story

1 "IT PAYS TO BE A WINNER"

On a rare chilly morning in the usual heat of Texas, a crying baby was born. Soft large blue eyes stared into those of his mother's eyes. His blonde newborn hair already slightly showing. After a couple of moments with mother and baby exchanging looks, the baby was quickly taken away by a nearby nurse. The baby was wrapped in a soft blanket and swiftly taken from the room in the arms of the nurse. The mother in tears, while staring as the nurse walks away, is quickly at peace.

A military couple, small statured woman and wife, Diane, and tall slender man and United States Air Force

Pilot Charlie, received a phone call from a case worker at the Texas Cradle Society telling them they would be parents. A blue eyed and blonde baby boy was ready to be picked up. Charlie called his team on base to notify them he would not be making his flights in the morning as he needed to pick up his new baby boy.

The next day, Diane and Charlie traveled to the Texas Cradle Society to pick up their new baby boy. Upon seeing him, Charlie and Diane both smiled. They looked down at the baby blue eyes and whisper, 'we shall call you, Doug'. Diane recalled the long journey to get Doug: background checks, home visits, training on how to parent an adoptee, and appointments with the adoption agency on preferred child criteria. Charlie and Diane wanted a child with blue eyes and blonde hair to help fit into the family. They waited a long period of time for a child they felt was a perfect match. Diane felt overwhelming joy and anxiety the day had arrived for their perfect child. The patience of waiting and finally meeting their child, "***it [paid] to be a winner***".

After admiring Doug, the three of them left to go home. Years flashed by with Doug quickly growing up as a healthy boy. Doug grew up in a calm and welcoming home. He experienced holidays, dressing up for Halloween, seeing his dad at work, and traveling to multiple places for family vacation.

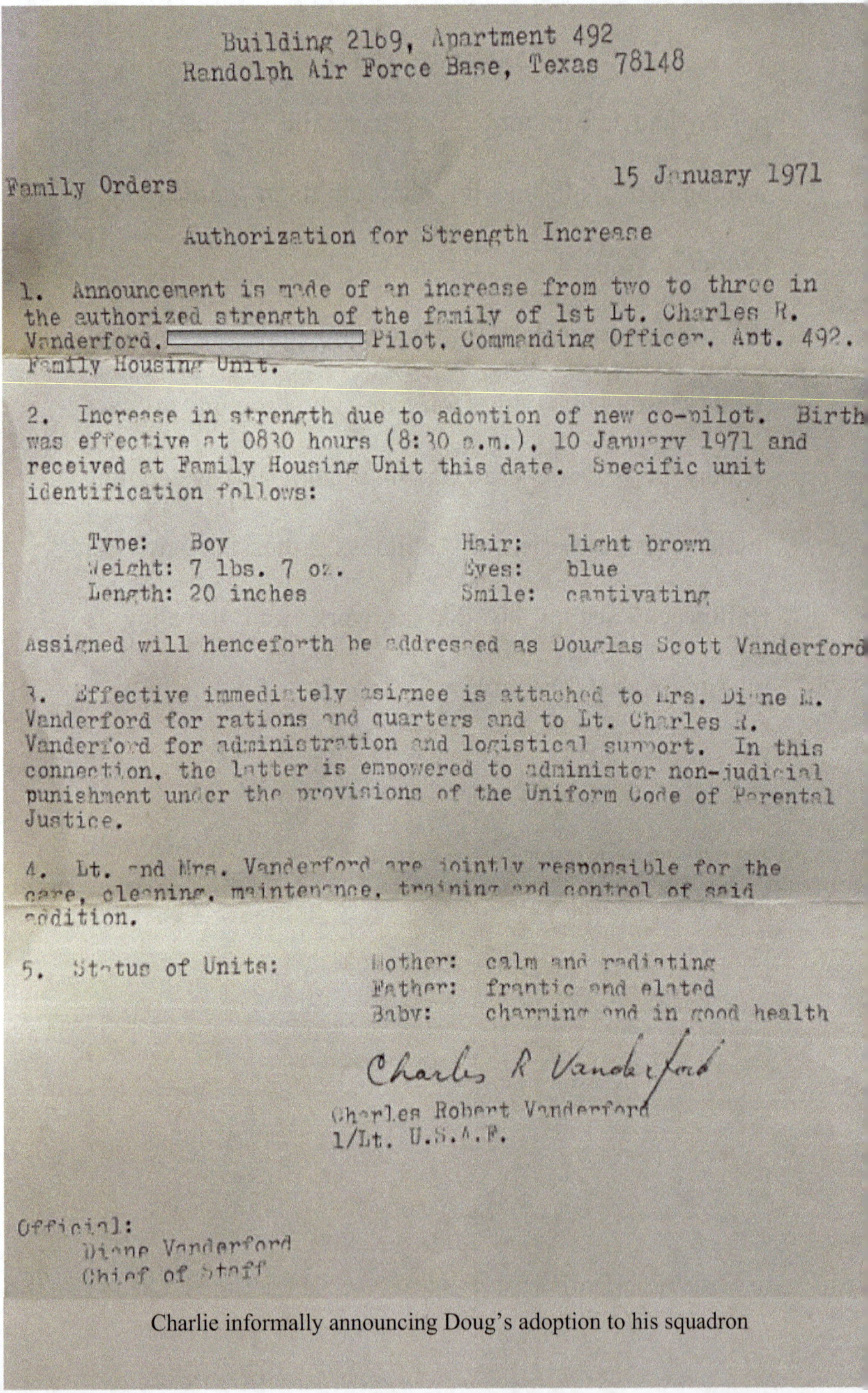

Building 2169, Apartment 492
Randolph Air Force Base, Texas 78148

Family Orders

15 January 1971

Authorization for Strength Increase

1. Announcement is made of an increase from two to three in the authorized strength of the family of 1st Lt. Charles R. Vanderford, [redacted] Pilot, Commanding Officer, Apt. 492, Family Housing Unit.

2. Increase in strength due to adoption of new co-pilot. Birth was effective at 0830 hours (8:30 a.m.), 10 January 1971 and received at Family Housing Unit this date. Specific unit identification follows:

Type:	Boy	Hair:	light brown
Weight:	7 lbs. 7 oz.	Eyes:	blue
Length:	20 inches	Smile:	captivating

Assigned will henceforth be addressed as Douglas Scott Vanderford

3. Effective immediately asignee is attached to Mrs. Diane M. Vanderford for rations and quarters and to Lt. Charles R. Vanderford for administration and logistical support. In this connection, the latter is empowered to administer non-judicial punishment under the provisions of the Uniform Code of Parental Justice.

4. Lt. and Mrs. Vanderford are jointly responsible for the care, cleaning, maintenance, training and control of said addition.

5. Status of Units:

Mother:	calm and radiating
Father:	frantic and elated
Baby:	charming and in good health

Charles R Vanderford

Charles Robert Vanderford
1/Lt. U.S.A.F.

Official:
Diane Vanderford
Chief of Staff

Charlie informally announcing Doug's adoption to his squadron

At age two, Diane and Charlie noticed a large red spot on Doug's right eye. Diane took Doug to the doctor. The red spot was non-life threatening but was suggested to be removed at a young age so it would not get bigger.

Diane was not ready to hear that her child needed surgery at such a young age, she thought, ***"nobody wants to hear the truth"*** when it pertains to their child needing surgery. However, Diane knew it was best for

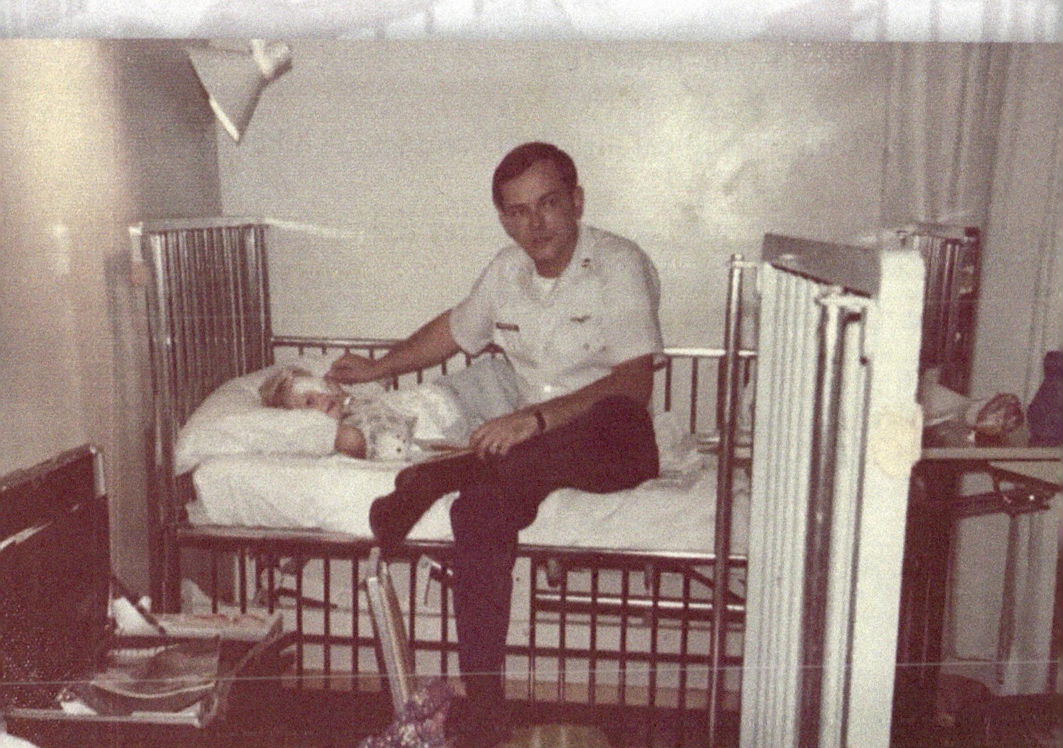

Doug (left) with Charlie (right) recovering from eye surgery

Doug to have the surgery so he could be comfortable, and the red spot would not get any bigger. Diane and Charlie scheduled an appointment and arrived at the hospital for Doug to have his eye surgery.

After a couple days of recovery in the hospital, Doug was able to open his eyes. He was excited to see his parents. Diane and Charlie were happy the surgery was a success. However, they realized his eye spot concern was one of many medical histories they would not have complete insight into. They had to learn from scratch about Doug's medical history. Diane felt a bit helpless not knowing his history so she could try to help prior to Doug facing the medical challenge.

2 "NOTHING LASTS FOREVER"

By age 3, Doug was spending most of his days playing outside, hitting and throwing baseballs, kicking soccer balls, and playing tag with his friends. While Doug was living the life of an average 3-year-old, Diane and Charlie were busy researching adoption agencies in their new hometown. They had decided it was time to bring another child into their family. This time, they were hoping for a little girl.

One day while playing outside with his friends, a random car drove up in front of their house. Doug stopped in his tracks and stared out to the car. Diane and Charlie quickly ran down to the car. Diane opened the backseat door. A little girl was picked up and placed in Diane's arms. The girl stared out and locked eyes with Doug from afar. Moments later, Diane carried the girl into their house. She then said to Doug, "meet your sister, Cara". Doug perked up, eyebrows raised, and confused, "sister!?", "what does that mean"? Diane explains, "a sister is a girl who will be part of our family. You will be her big

Doug (middle) with his sister Cara (left) and Charlie (right)

brother". Doug thought he would be the only child forever but quickly realized, "**nothing lasts forever**". Doug was sad that Diane and Charlie would no longer give him all the attention, having to share with Cara, but he accepted he would have to grow up and be a good big brother.

Days passed and Doug warmed up to the idea of having a sister. He quickly realized Cara did not look like him – she had auburn hair and brown eyes. Doug led the way in teaching Cara how to play.

He spent time with Cara watching cartoons, teaching her hopscotch, how to ride a bicycle, playing with her dolls, play tag, grow chia pets at home, and even how to play the sports he loved. Doug loved being a big brother. He got a full-time friend and got to lead aka "boss around someone".

In the coming years, Doug and his family had to move many times due to Charlie's job in the military. The family realized home is where the Air Force sent you. Often, Diane, was left to take care of Doug and Cara by herself. Charlie, serving in the military as a pilot, would fly many training sessions away from home.

Doug did not mind having to move to new locations. He easily made friends with new people and made more friends to play his favorite sports with. He spent most of his time playing baseball, soccer, and football in the new countries. When Doug was around 10 years old, Charlie came home and let the family know they would be moving to Germany for his next military assignment. Upon hearing Doug had to move to Germany, he was scared. Doug thought about his history classes of World War II and the Holocaust and those times where many adults and children were harmed. Doug talked to Charlie about his fear of moving to such a dangerous location. Charlie compassionate but stern words **“get comfortable being uncomfortable”**, “you will be safe, Doug”.

Doug and the rest of the family moved to Germany. While living in Germany for 3 years, Doug met many new friends. He signed up for the local Air Force base youth baseball team. Doug felt lucky to play with his team on the ballfield which was near the Berlin Wall (years prior to its fall in November 1989). The wall was covered in a mixture of vibrant graffiti and baseball imprints from hitting the balls on the solid concrete. Doug spent most of his days after school running to the baseball field, excitedly waiting to hang out with his friends. He made it known he wanted to be a team captain. He spent many hours off the field practicing becoming the best athlete. He knew he could not be a captain if he did not put the extra hours in to improve himself.

He wanted to be a role model to others, of working hard and being trustworthy and motivating his team. When the team was losing or in a slump, Doug would be the first to remind them, ***"Stay positive. Stay fighting. Stay brave. Stay ambitious. Stay focused. Stay strong".*** Doug was a born leader and loved taking charge.

Charlie (left) and Doug (middle front row) in Germany with their baseball team

One day, Doug noticed things about his friend's parents picking up their kids from practice. He stared at the resemblance, the kids looked identical to their parents and siblings. Doug reflecting on his own personal appearance to his parents and sister. Doug sprinted home from the baseball field. Doug searched through the house looking for Diane. Upon finding her, he looked up to his mom with his blue eyes and asked, "why do I look different from you, dad, and Cara?" His mom stared at him and smiled. Diane asked Doug to find his sister and to come to the kitchen. Shortly thereafter, the family sat together at the dining table. Diane and Charlie both explain to Doug and Cara that they were adopted. Doug was puzzled, having heard the word "adopted" before but not understanding what it meant. His mom explains, "adoption is when a child gets a family that gives them a home and love while not being physically born from the mom and dad. We are a family by love, not related by blood." Doug takes a moment to process and replies, "so it means you love us even if we are not biologically yours?" His mom smiling and replying, "yes, exactly!" Doug smiled back, "that's cool, more kids should be adopted!"

For years following the adoption conversation, Doug did not think often about his adoption situation. He was content with having family that was not related to him. However, his sister, Cara, would question Doug why he was not interested in his biological family. Frustrated, Cara would question why Doug was curious but did not want to know why his biological mom gave him up, his family medical history, whether he had other siblings, who his looks most resemble, feeling of judgement for not looking like his adopted family, and/or if his biological parents regret giving him up? She had all these questions of her own biological parents and struggled with internally. The most important question whether Diane and Charlie loved both as their own, even if not biologically related? Doug thought over Cara's questions and concerns but did not care to know the answers. Letting Cara know, "***it's all mind over matter, if I don't mind, then it doesn't matter".***

Doug was content with his situation and adoptive parents. Doug let Diane and Charlie know he had no intentions to look for his biological parents.

Diane and Charlie would often ask Doug if he wanted to look for his biological parents. They would be willing to help him search. They wanted to keep the door open for whatever information and contact he wanted to explore regarding his biological parents. Doug often reminded Diane and Charlie that they were his parents. He felt the love they gave him since leaving the Texas Cradle

Society as a baby and never questioned whether there could be more if he was biologically related. He felt chosen by them.

3 "LIFE IS JUDGED, LIFE IS TIMED"

For most Doug's life, he moved from one military base to another whenever Charlie received a new mission assignment. In his high school years Doug moved to Florida. He continued to play many sports. Doug was a high school star athlete, playing football and soccer. Doug loved high school. He blossomed into a charming young man with the right pick-up lines to get girls to talk to him.

Doug had many friends to hang out with. Whichever sport he played he was often the sports team captain, leading and motivating his teams. He passed his classes with little effort. He was confident in his athletic and academic abilities. The world seemed easy and straightforward. Doug was ready for the next step in his life, college.

Doug enrolled in college and found it was difficult. He spent many late nights and days trying to study, with little discipline. He struggled to understand the topics and hated every single moment of college. He could not see his future of where he would be in life. There was no purpose or passion, but just daily routine of waking up, attending class, homework, and repeat. He felt miserable in college and felt like his purpose was elsewhere.

Doug pushed through two years of college and received his two-year associates degree. However, he did not want to spend another miserable day in college. Doug was afraid of what his parents would think of him if he dropped out of college. It was considered most direct route to finding a good job. Doug began self-reflecting, questioning his existence and purpose in life. Life had to be more than just getting a degree and a job.

One day after visiting Charlie, Doug reflected on his

Doug as an infant with his dad prior to a flight mission

dad's military career. The multiple missions overseas, the soldiers he met on each base, military family events, attendance of airshows with Charlie pointing out which pilot friend was in the aircraft at the time, retirement and promotion ceremonies, and countless amount of salutes Charlie received. Doug asked Charlie why he joined the military. Charlie told Doug the military gave him purpose in life. It allowed him to be part of a team, lead others, and provide for his family. He was able to coach and mentor soldiers during hardships, work with a team to get families home safely during wartimes while also getting to explore new states and countries. Charlie felt commitment to his surrounding servicemen, and their families, knowing they could depend on him to get his team home safely while also inspiring them to lead.

Charlie was grateful for his time in the military and the multiple missions he was given. He was even more grateful that it allowed him the chance to adopt Doug.

Doug listening to Charlie realized the magnitude of purpose the military gives to oneself, and to serve the country above self. Still afraid of the judgement from his parents of dropping out of college, Doug quit and notified Diane and Charlie he planned to the military. Doug anticipated the disgrace upon his announcement,

Doug visiting Charlie prior to a flight mission in a T-38A

with Charlie and Diane exchanging wisdom, ***"life is judged, life is timed,"*** each person should live the life that gives them purpose, not based on what others think one should do. Doug realized his parents were open to whatever life decisions he wanted for himself. They would support him, like they had from the day they adopted him. They were as open about his life decisions as they were about his adoption. Doug felt happiness and great pride to join the military.

Doug recalled his childhood of dressing up as a military serviceman for Halloween, and the overwhelming honor when he heard United States national anthem played at events. He knew joining the military was his calling and purpose. Doug wanted to be like his dad and give back to his country.

Doug was ready to join the military. He thought long and hard about which military branch; follow in his dad's footsteps and join the Air Force, or go elsewhere? Doug decided to join the United States Navy. He wanted to be a part of an elite group that would challenge him mentally and physically, every day. A group that had mission and purpose every waking moment. The United States Navy Special Operations.

4 "TOUGHNESS INVOLVES HAVING CONTROL OVER YOUR THOUGHTS & EMOTIONS"

Doug challenged himself preparing for bootcamp like he did for his sports growing up. He studied for his Armed Services Vocational Aptitude Battery (ASVAB) test ensuring he would academically be qualified for the opportunity to compete for a spot in the Special Operations group. He spent months improving his physical fitness by practicing his running, swimming, push-ups, sit-ups, and pull-ups. He wanted to be the best. He knew "***toughness involves having control over your thoughts***" and excelling at Navy bootcamp and qualifying for Special Operations would require mental and physical strength.

The day arrived, Doug packed up and left home to attend bootcamp at Naval Station Great Lakes in North Chicago, Illinois. Doug arrived late at night. As soon as he took a step off the base transportation bus, multiple instructors yelled at him to run, stay quiet and listen to instructions. This was the first of many weeks of constant yelling and stress. Doug stayed mentally motivated despite the constant exhaustion due to early morning wake up calls and long days. He embraced the challenge of swimming in a 12 feet deep pool, motivating his team in abandoned ship scenarios, operating fire weapons safely and calmly braving the gas chamber learning chemical, biological and radiological hazards, learning firefighter tactics, and enduring 12-hour battle station attack simulation.

Doug quickly stood out as a natural leader during

bootcamp and rewarded with being named a battalion guidon bearer. The battalion's guidon bearer alerts the General of the unit's positioning within battle. It is used in marching formation and represented the lead person, standing tall with the battalion commander.

After 9 weeks of training Doug graduated bootcamp, Doug stayed in Great Lakes, Illinois to advance to his next phase of training: Interior Communications basic and advanced courses. He was eager to get through the screening phases of training to maintain his competition placeholder for the Special Operations group.

Doug was mentally overwhelmed with the amount of information he had to retain but this was different than college. He had purpose. Each day, he was faced with increasing challenges. He realized each day "***will be the hardest thing [he will] have ever done, but it is not impossible. You keep your head down, move forward,***

and* never *quit." To reach his overall purpose and goal of Special Operations, he could not quit. He had to face whatever challenge was presented to him. Doug learned the responsibilities maintaining all the ship's communication systems. He learned about the installation and repair of U.S Navy ship interior communication systems, including navigation system, visual aids for aircraft and warning systems. He had to make sure interior communications were maintained, telecommunication systems were installed and configured, navigation equipment and operating systems were functioning, and supported the systems engineering department in maintaining of the ship's wiring.

Upon learning the basics of ship communication systems, Doug was rewarded with advanced training, learning gyrocompass (compass determining direction of ship based on earth's rotation) and advanced visual maintenance. After nearly 6 months of communication training, Doug was happy to graduate and get his first Naval assignment.

SWCC Designator Pin

5 "YOU ONLY GOT THREE CHOICES IN LIFE: GIVE UP, GIVE IN, OR GIVE IT ALL YOU'VE GOT"

Upon graduating Basic and Advanced Interior Communication school, Doug was stationed at the United States Pentagon in Arlington, Virginia, near Washington D.C working Special Program Details. Doug felt anxious having not yet been accepted into the Special Operations training. He started questioning his choice of joining the military. For the first time in the military, he felt out of place. It was the same feelings he once felt when realizing he was adopted and his time in college. Was this what his military career would come down to, maintaining communication systems for the Navy and any other vessel he would be assigned? He had worked hard to be the best. To stay physically and mentally fit. To stand out as a leader. He had many internal talks with himself and realized, ***"you've only got three choices in life: give up, give in, or give it all you've got".*** To mentally question the tasking is giving up. He needed to press on and make the most of it. He recalled that his father had been stern about being comfortable in uncomfortable situations. This was the adult version of embracing non-ideal situations. Doug promised himself to buckle down and give it all he had.

Soon after Doug's internal emotional battle of fitting in to the Navy, he received the call he had been waiting for, he was assigned to attend the Navy's Special Operations, Special Warfare Combatant-Craft Crewman

(SWCC) training. He packed up his gear and traveled from Virginia to Naval Base Coronado-Naval Amphibious Base in San Diego, California.

Doug arrived at SWCC training excited and nervous. Doug quickly realized the instructors there were 20 times more intense than the ones he faced in bootcamp or any place elsewhere. The days started and ended in the dark. He had daily thoughts of whether he would survive. Almost every day someone would ring “The Bell” or drop-on-request (DOR), signifying a fellow candidate quitting SEAL training. While training in 52-degree water in the California ocean during numerous exercises, Doug too questioned quitting. The instructors screamed in each person’s face close enough to see each wrinkle and freckle. This was not at all what Doug expected. Heavy thoughts of how much longer of this misery as he was constantly reminded by the instructors, **“you don’t ever**

let quitting enter your mind as it is a sickness that will weaken you". Maybe they were right, Doug thought, the less I think of quitting, the more I stay focused to the mission and completing this. Afterall, **"nobody remembers a loser or a quitter".** Doug endured multiple individual and team physical tests including swimming oceans, pushups, sit-ups, pullups,

Figure 1: DIVIDS

SWCC navigates a MarkV (back) with 11M rigid-hull inflatable during training

and obstacle courses. He was challenged to become familiar with boat operations, navigating day and night. Doug was proud to be 1 of 77 sailors to attend SWCC training, and 1 of 17 to graduate after 4 months of grueling physical and mental challenges, in class #25.

Upon graduating SWCC, Doug went to Warner Springs for Survival, Evasion, Resistance, and Escape (SERE) training in San Diego, California. Doug spent over a month learning basic skills to survive simulated missions of search and rescue, evading captures of hostile forces (surviving captivity), and surviving starvation. Doug quickly realized SWCC school was a dress rehearsal for Advanced United Level Training (AULT). He was quickly being trained to be physically and mentally broken down. He faced what Prisoner of War (POW) persons endure and being isolated without food and water. Doug soon realized as training advanced ***"the only easy day was yesterday".***

Upon graduating SERE, Doug attended Advanced Unit Training (AUT) with Special Boat Unit 20 at Naval Amphibious Base in Little Creek, Norfolk, Virginia. Doug was trained in advanced combat medicine, counterintelligence, surveillance, airborne jump, and free fall school (including aerial maneuvers). During jump school, Doug quickly realized the importance of following directions so it would not result in a severe or deadly situation for both him and his teammates. There was no room for mistakes before, during and after training. "***There are two ways to do something … the right way, and again***".

While the training was mentally and physically demanding, for the first time, Doug felt like he fit in. He saw daily individual and team missions. If he could not pull his weight to support the team, it would impact the outcome, severely. He had to hold himself accountable to

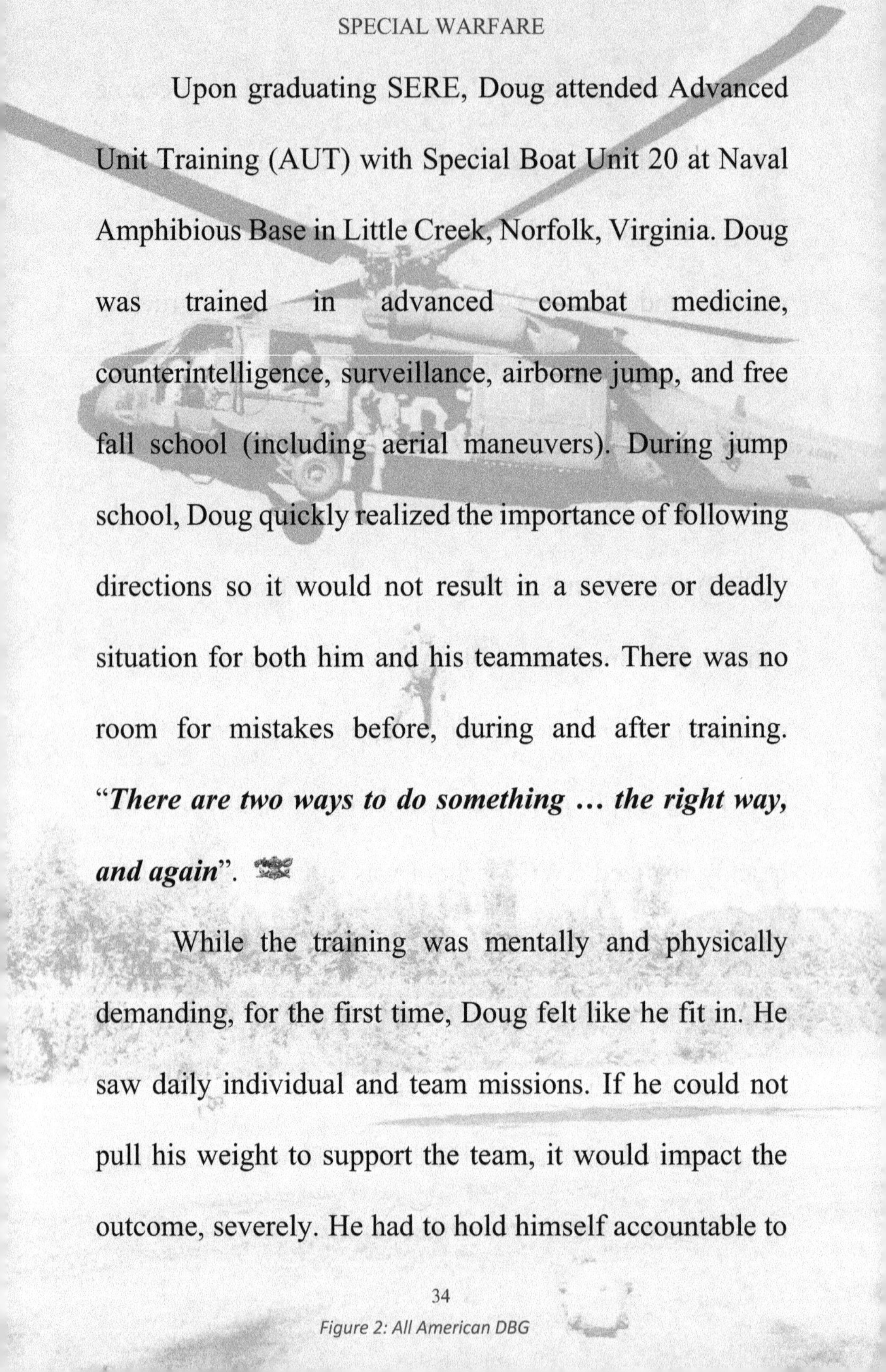

Figure 2: All American DBG

train harder, get smarter, and think strategically. Mistakes are not options as a crewman who support SEALS and Special Forces groups. After finishing AUT, Doug proudly earned his SWCC designator. A premier qualification showcasing recognition and ability to operate within advanced tactical teams. Without any break in between training, Doug spent 16 months alongside the Navy SEAL platoon that he would deploy with.

He worked through wartime simulations with his teams to learn the designated boat maneuvering and operations, water diving, usage of weapons, tactic deployments, and running simulated mission operations in expected deployment environments. Doug's assigned Special Boat Team 20 (SBT-20) would simulate missions to include crewmen landing in open water from a C-130 Hercules airplane via Maritime Craft Air Deployable System (MCADS), firing a machine gun from a rigid-hull inflatable boat (RHIB), hooking up boat slings on helicopters, and deployment approaches to get Navy SEALS to and from missions.

Figure 3: All American DBG

SEALS conducting a maritime training exercise with SWCC Special Boat Team using a MH-47G Chinook helicopter

6 "SAY GOODNIGHT TO THE SUN"

One day during SEAL and SWCC operation training, Doug was called over by a cadre member. Doug ran over and was told to sit down. Doug was puzzled, not knowing what he did wrong to be called into the instructor's office. Doug was told he would be deploying. He needed to pack up as soon as possible and was given his deployment orders. One of the deployed SWCC members was injured in action and Doug had the right skills to replace him.

The cadre released Doug and armed him with "***say goodnight to the sun***." Doug packed his items and caught a flight out to Iraq. His thoughts were running 100 miles an hour as was his heart. He was nervous to deploy. Doug trained multiple years for deployment but did not expect to go months ahead of the original schedule.

Doug landed in Iraq and was shocked at what he saw. The desert was dry, lonely, and many of his friends and teammates killed in combat. The longer he was out

Doug (left) with his SBT-20 team.

there, the higher importance he saw to work with his teammates to come back safely to base each day. The number of teammates missing in action trumped the amount of coming home. Each day in Iraq challenged Doug on his combat skills. He realized he could only train so much in the United States but being out in real life or death combat would be the ultimate test and training, ***"you'll never know your limits until you push yourself to them."***

Doug served 4 deployments with SBT-20. After 8 years in the U.S Navy, Doug felt the impact of the years of training and deployments. His body was slowly beaten by the constant weight of equipment, jumping out of aircraft, hard forces of boat operations on unforgiving water conditions, and being away from his family. Doug fulfilled his existing contract and was honorably discharged.

While serving in the Navy, Doug felt the purpose he was seeking when he felt lost during his college years. He enjoyed working alongside mentally and physically strong individuals, leading teams and giving to a mission that was bigger than himself. He felt joy in helping others become better versions of themselves and creating common excellence to help his teammates come home to their families.

Doug too had a sense of purpose to come home safely. During his time in the Navy, he got married and became a father. Doug felt and lived many of the emotions he recalled his father talking about nearly a decade earlier, the honor of being able to work with his fellow teammates to accomplish a mission and get families home safely.

As Doug reflected on his time in the Navy, he found that being adopted helped his mental state and successes in the military. He realized growing up and accepting his situation as an adoptee and not dwelling on missing out helped him stay focused in his military challenges. To focus on what he had versus what he did not. To be thankful for the equipment he was given that would satisfy the training rather than what he did not have. His ability to lead and work with others when they were lost. To mentally navigate oneself without pre-defined expectations but understanding the main

Doug holding his son in front of MKV and Z-birds (zodiac inflatable boats)

mission and adapting. And sometimes not knowing every detail of your past can be better to open your mind of possibilities within yourself and team.

THE END

POST NAVY/SWCC

Once Doug left the military, he continued seeking life's purpose and his goal to achieve mission excellence bigger than himself. He was hired by Blackwater in North Carolina as a military contractor to train servicemen to respond with urgency to remove threats in military combat zones. After multiple years of training personnel with dynamic live fire, he was hired as a Subject Matter Expert working operations and training techniques for ITA (In the Arena) in Norfolk, Virginia.

Doug spent 12 years as a staff lead to train nearly

10,000 sailors, both active and reservist, working with 3 Navy SEALS and 3 SWCC Dynamic Live Fire Range Officers developing tactics, techniques, and procedures for Navy units. He trained the sailors to "***hold fast, stay true***" in unpredicted times while trusting the training.

Most of the training, techniques, procedures, and operating standards Doug helped create through ITA are still used today. Doug spent most of each year, 200 days, traveling across the country sometimes pulling 16-hour days for 3 straight weeks, a schedule he was intimately familiar with during his SWCC training and deployments. After a decade of spending long days and weeks training thousands of sailors, Doug was ready to settle down and limit his working hours and travel. In 2018, he submitted his resignation.

When Doug left his physically and mentally demanding career, he became a substitute teacher for a year, teaching multiple topics to K-12th graders and traveling with his significant other, Lisa Zaranek.

Holding himself accountable and finishing what you start, Doug went back to college and finished his bachelor's degree. He then got hired at a Department of Defense contract company where he leads teams as a Project Manager.

Doug credits his adoption and loving family to his decades of service to the United States military. He grew up with a loving family who was open about his adoption and instilling in him a sense of duty to serve for others. His sense of pride was a driving force in working with teams to bring his colleagues back home safely to their families. He did not want others to face the lack of family, nor want young children to face a day without their parents.

Doug experienced ultimate servant leadership through his adoptive parents, providing for and loving another child as their own. Each day Doug lives out, he is instilling compassion and leadership to others so they can provide to missions bigger than themselves. While Doug did not join the Air Force and follow exactly in his dad's steps, he felt the same great pride his dad shared with him from his infant age and into adulthood. Doug and Charlie both reminisce their times in the military and how Doug's adoption created purpose for both Doug and Charlie, and future generations.

Doug with his family, Charlie (left), Diane, Daphne (daughter), and Lisa

SWCC CREED

In our nation's time of need, an elite group of maritime warriors stands ready off distant shores and on shallow rivers. Defending freedom, they serve with honor and distinction. I am proud to be one of these Sailors.

I am a Special Warfare Combatant-craft Crewman: a quiet professional; tried, tested and dedicated to achieving excellence in maritime special operations. I am a disciplined, confident and highly motivated warrior.

My honor and integrity are beyond reproach, my commitment unquestioned and my word trusted. The American people depend on me to carry out my mission in a professional manner.

I maintain my craft, equipment and myself at the highest level combat readiness. I set the standard and lead by example. I am responsible for my actions and accountable to my teammates. I challenge them to perform, as I expect them to challenge me.

I am ready for war. I will close and engage the enemy with the full combat power of my craft. My actions will be decisive yet measured. I will always complete the mission. I will never quit and I will leave no one behind.

My heritage comes from the Sailors who operated the PT boats of World War II and the combatant craft of Vietnam. The legacy of these warriors guides my actions. I will always remember the courage, perseverance and sacrifices made to guarantee our nation's freedom. I uphold the honor of those who have fought before me and will do nothing to disgrace my proud heritage,

On Time, On Target, Never Quit

nsw.navy.mil/

SPECIAL WARFARE

SPECIAL WARFARE

SPECIAL WARFARE

SPECIAL WARFARE

SPECIAL WARFARE

SPECIAL WARFARE

SPECIAL WARFARE

www.ingramcontent.com/pod-product-compliance
Lightning Source LLC
LaVergne TN
LVHW010358160826
845677LV00005BA/1312
* 9 7 9 8 3 6 8 0 3 6 7 3 1 *